Odysseus to Athena
Sonnets from the Greek

by
Sidney Krome

PublishAmerica
Baltimore

© 2003 by Sidney Krome.
All rights reserved. No part of this book may be reproduced, stored in a retrieval system, or transmitted in any form or by any means without the prior written permission of the publishers, except by a reviewer who may quote brief passages in a review to be printed in a newspaper, magazine, or journal.

First printing

ISBN: 1-4137-0608-8
PUBLISHED BY PUBLISHAMERICA, LLLP
www.publishamerica.com
Baltimore

Printed in the United States of America

AUTHOR'S NOTES:

Throughout the poems, I use the Greek names as transliterated by Robert Fitzgerald (minus the accent marks) in his translation of *The Odyssey* originally published in 1961 by Doubleday.

"Odysseus to Athena" and "The Goddess Forsakes Odysseus" were originally published in THE PAPER (Baltimore) in December 1971.

FOR MY WIFE

SOPHIA MASTROS KROME:

Πρόσ τήν Ἀθηνά

ACKNOWLEDGEMENTS

For the inspiration for these poems, I acknowledge the gifts of *Athena*, without whose loving encouragement, protection, and support Odysseus would never have returned from Troy; of *Homer*, without whose creative genius there would have been no *Odyssey* and thus no still-living tale of Odysseus and Athena to be read; of *Robert Fitzgerald*, without whose poetic genius there would have been no worthy English *Odyssey* to touch my heart with the tale of Odysseus and Athena; and of *my wife Sophia Mastros Krome*, without whose loving inspiration there would be no still-living tale of Odysseus and Athena for me to have written.

CONTENTS

PROLOGUE: ODYSSEUS TO ATHENA 13
THE SONNETS 19
    THE COUNCIL OF THE GODS 21
    KALYPSO 22
    THE RAFT 23
    NAUSIKAA 24
    SKHERIA: MIST 25
    DEMODOKOS 26
    KIKONES 27
    LOTOS EATERS 28
    KYKLOPS 29
    AIOLOS 30
    LAISTRYGONES 31
    KIRKE 32
    HADES: TEIRESIAS 33
    HADES: AGAMEMNON 34
    HADES: AKHILLEUS 35
    SEIRENES 36
    PLANKTAS 37
    SKYLLA 38
    HELIOS' CATTLE 39
    KHARYBDIS 40

RETURN TO ITHAKA 41
EUMAIOS' HUT: REUNION WITH
   TELEMAKHOS 42
THE BEGGAR 43
THE WARRIOR'S CLOTHING 44
EURYKLEIA: THE SCAR 45
PENELOPE'S CUNNING: THE BOW 46
THE SLAUGHTER OF THE SUITORS . . . 47
THE PURGING OF THE HALL 48
THE OLIVE TREE BED 49
LAERTES AND HIS LINE 50
VICTORY 51
PEACE FROM THE GODS 52
EPILOGUE: THE GODDESS FORSAKES
   ODYSSEUS 55

PROLOGUE:

ODYSSEUS TO ATHENA

Aghia, Aghia,
my Athena dark eyes –
not glittering, not bright –
dark –

Where brown becomes black,
no iris or pupil,
a variation in shades:
one the blood fresher, still soaking,
the other richer, absorbed, more fertile;
my eyes, my feet, plunged in
nerve deep;
crushing the walls of my earth-needing veins,
the bubbling blood-lava flows, expands,
fills my once air-filled muscles,
gives me strength beyond deception.

Clothe me not in mists, that my eyes see
while my body becomes an intangible puff;
I'll enter neither the world
 nor you
as a cold and clammy fume;
no more my namesake, nor you yours –
though thus I call you –
I'll be no longer a shape-shifter,
the wily one, full of cunning,

to grin and rub my hands
at being no-name:
let me take form!

Out of the earth of your eyes,
I draw my strength, my shape;
Antaean I'll be, and you my source;
no sly one – myself or another –
to break the bond:
in sight or out, I am in your eyes,
buried to mine;
the pressure cools my skin, tempers my flesh;
in the blood-dark grave of your eyes
I cannot decompose:
you resurrect me:
not my spirit, my mind –
me.

Ysigheia, Aghia,
my Athena dark eyes –
not bright, not glittering –
blood-rich earth –
dark –

THE SONNETS

THE COUNCIL OF THE GODS

In bright Olympos' hall did Zeus retell
Aigisthos' fate: with grief for me you rose
to help my soul escape Kalypso's cell;
Poseidon's wrath for Kyklops' eye my woes
had caused, but could not blunt my fate: to home
I'd go: the gods resolved to heed your words.
To men whose empty lives recount the knell
of doom, I speak as one who living knows:
my heart has drunk from grieving's salty well,
and eye has seen the pain that struggle shows:
their soul is mine without your loving poem:
by love resolved, to them I speak my words.
With grief you spoke to gods to end my strife,
to men I speak of love that gives me life.

KALYPSO

From seaward eyes I wept a tide of tears:
Penelope I sought, though she must die;
Kalypso's grace, immortal form, for years
had sapped my strength and will; long sated, I
for wife's warm flesh, soon cold, did yearn: a man,
no life I felt without contending trials.
Your goddess body stills my mortal fears:
beside your spirit flesh at home I lie,
and feel the flood of strength that surging veers
from you; and though the falcon years will fly
and leave us cold in our embrace, I can
contend with loving life's enduring trials.
Kalypso's love my self from life withdrew,
but you my soul to living's world renew.

THE RAFT

The bitter sea beyond Kalypso's isle
to cross, a raft of twenty trees I made:
alone with fear, I watched an endless file
of days and waves; Poseidon's wrath delayed
no more: for three full days, my raft destroyed,
I fought the storm and body-crushing sea.
As wild a sea today I face, yet smile:
aboard the raft of you, with sighs I've prayed
for cresting waves that I – no arms or guile
to help – might ride, my strength my only aid,
and naked limbs: I plunge, my body buoyed
by you, through love's unending stormy sea.
My water-battered body fought for shore,
now me you float, and calm the sea once more.

NAUSIKAA

Nausikaa's ball you sent to find my lair:
and I – a sodden, clotted mass, with brine
and blood all crust, and weed-entangled hair –
came forth; her eyes reached out to mine:
though food I took, and drink, her maiden's hands
I stopped: alone – with you – I hid to bathe.
Through seas of days I swim, my body bare
to salting waves and bleeding rocks: a sign,
your eyes now show me shelter I can share:
the bread of you I eat, and drink your wine;
and cast ashore from swims to distant lands
my crusted skin with goddess' hands you bathe.
My weathered flesh, once hid from maiden view,
now stands refreshed by cleansing touch of you.

SKHERIA: MIST

Your cunning matched my own: though I this land
with salt-burned eyes could see, my well-known face
in mist so fine you clad that who would stand
and gaze a hazy whiteness in my place
would see: the rocks and olive trees beyond
would penetrate my non-existent form.
Now you in mist I clothe, a pure-white band
no eye can pierce but mine, though hazy lace
it be and clear; my eye shall be my hand,
my gaze your body, not a cloud, embrace;
between the two this vision molds a bond:
with mortal eyes I see your goddess form.
From lurking eyes my presence you concealed,
to loving eyes your being stands revealed.

DEMODOKOS

The woes of Troy the minstrel's song recalled:
Akhilleus' anger raged with mine once more
as softened sobs I cried; in tears, enthralled,
my eyes the wooden horse through Trojan door
to Trojan doom beheld: thus moved, I named
my self and told my many-voyaged tale.
With love, not guile, have you my heart unwalled;
now mused by you I sing our loving lore:
the clash of anger stills, when softly called
to softness turns; and raging passion's war
by opened arms and bodies soon is tamed:
with love I tell our many-ventured tale.
Though minstrel's visions bade me, longing, weep,
in treasured tales of us my life I steep.

KIKONES

From Troy with booty's pride and hearts of lust
for blood we sailed: Kikones' land our thirst
would quench; we stormed their place, our raid a gust
of plund'ring wind; but greed our party cursed:
Kikones blew with gales upon my men,
left beaches strewn with dead beside their loot.
With loving greed I plunder you, and must:
my passion's wind unblown, my heart would burst
from holding back the storm; and you I trust
to plunder me with equal force; thus nursed
in blood's desire we raid ourselves again,
our beach awash with love that is our loot.
The grief that came from greed for plunder's gold
you turn to loving booty that we hold.

LOTOS EATERS

In wrath the thunder god a rage of night
blew down: we furled our sails, held oars in hand;
set free, for days through gales we had to fight,
then beached where Lotos Eaters lived – like sand
their lives through feebled fingers sift: to grief
and hope the Lotos fed a deadly peace.
When wind and waves of darkness' rage ignite
the fires of pain, and hope for homeland's strand
grows dim, I toil my ship to lee and, tight
with straining, beach on you: then from your land
I pluck and eat your Lotos, root and leaf,
and feed upon your strength-renewing peace.
The flow'r whose feeding dulled its eaters' strife
now feeds to me your honeyed plant of life.

KYKLOPS

Compassion grows from strange events: long years
have passed since I my bold and hardy crew
with brutal guile from Kyklops' raging tears
set free; his socket bloody black, he threw
huge rocks while bleating sheep and I in scorn
our voices joined: how proudly flashed my eyes!
Yet now, alone, I stumble through my fears,
my single-sighted vision less than true;
since you are gone, bare half of all that nears
I see – my other eye belongs to you:
a Kyklops I – though man with two eyes born –
have need of both your shining goddess eyes.
The Kyklops, drunk, to darkness did awake,
the loss of you would be my blinding stake.

AIOLOS

Aiolos' gift was gold to me: in bullock's hide
his airs he bagged – the tempest's howl and crack
of storm – and bade me sail the Western tide
with ease; in sight of shore my hand went slack,
I slept; awake no land I saw: in greed
my men with knives had freed the wracking winds.
No air of life or love I fear: I ride
the gales of fortune's blows, take up the slack
of snapping sails; through hurricanes I glide,
of passion's storms, my tiller firm and back
unbent: for you mid storms and gale have freed
my Western tide, your gentle, easing winds.
My ship, that once the storms to havoc blew,
now sails the seas becalmed by winds of you.

LAISTRYGONES

My wit was with me then: my ship I moored
beyond the bay, the cove my squadron sought,
deceptive calm; of three I sent who toured
the rocky crags but two returned – one fought
the jaws of Laistrygones' king and lost:
my crew alone escaped that grisly feast.
No calmness holds me back, my hunger lured
inside the coves of you: my mouth is caught
by scent of flesh, and on my tongue I hoard
your taste: a Laistrygon to be I'm taught
by you, and relish feeding back the cost:
we savor each our loving hungers' feast.
My men in pain the savage giants fed,
but we in love to passion's food are led.

KIRKE

What wicked craft sweet Kirke's spells possessed
my men and I soon felt: as swine a year
of days and nights we spent entranced, caressed
by food and wine and witching ways; no tear
we shed but swilled and drank our souls' content:
till longing's pain dissolved her magic charms.
Against the lure of swinish life, distressed,
alone, I strain, of mind and soul in fear
bereft; temptation's wiles cast life unblessed,
bewitch its teeming joys from laugh to leer;
till you my soul entrance, my mind's consent,
and longing now I seek your loving charms.
What Kirke then with witch's woes accursed,
have you each day with lover's balms reversed.

HADES: TEIRESIAS

My ship to North I tilled in bitter dread:
to votive pit of blood Teiresias' shade
came forth, mid surge of fleshless phantom dead;
my sword I sheathed: he drank to speak and bade
me heed: where men no salt or oar can know
a sacrifice Poseidon's wrath demands.
To distant pit of you by love I'm led:
except I drink your blood my soul would fade
to shapeless shade; my quenchless thirst thus fed,
my used-up body flesh again is made:
wherever beating blood of mine does flow,
it speaks your name as jealous love demands.
The prophet's shade drank blood the truth to speak,
your blood that gives my body voice I seek.

HADES: AGAMEMNON

Through empty shades of Agamemnon's arms
my body slipped: he cried, the Argive King;
no soldier's end he met, sweet battle's charms,
nor storm at sea; his dying was a bitter thing,
as death itself: to wife's hot blade the throat
of ox, his blood she shed in welcome home.
No grim foreboding my return alarms:
I come from raging seas that loudly sing
of doom, and fields where battle grimly farms
for crops of men; no shade, I laurels bring,
from life hard-won: in your strong arms I float
as flow of love you shed in welcome home.
The King's enfeebled shade was shamed by wife,
with you I share the pride of striving's life.

HADES: AKHILLEUS

Akhilleus' feeble shade in Hades bore
a weight I held in awe: yet when my hand
his emptiness enclosed, he scorned me more
than I deserved: a plow on barren land
was gold to scepters wielded here; but I
his strength renewed: I told him of his son.
My weary shade betrays within a core
of emptiness: the sceptered life I'd planned
grows less than I deserve; but you restore
my strength: or thus in death forlorn I'd stand,
a weightless, imaged man; through you have I
my life renewed: you give to me a son.
In death the hero's shade had lost his worth,
this son you give foreshadows my rebirth.

SEIRENES

A sudden calm: my men all swiftness furled
the sails, with wax I thickly plugged their ears;
though lashed to mast, my self I would have hurled
to doom: from me Seirenes' voices tears
of longing drew: their lovely shivered shriek
of winds I heard, enticing madness' song.
Becalmed or blown, I row and sail a world
of seas: your voice with soothing quells my fears
of wind and foam; my sail I set unfurled,
through oceans plow: from shores your singing nears,
and wafts in waves to longing ears that seek
the lilting sound of love's uplifting song.
The lure of drowning seized me bound in rope,
now freed am I, enticed by you to hope.

PLANKTAS

The sea in turmoil smote the air: mid boom
of thrashing winds and smoke of billowed waves
the craggy rocks together clashed: a tomb
for men and ships; my own to watered graves
had sunk, their oars by trembling hands set free,
but them to courage I recalled with words.
The crash of passion's wind and wave no gloom
portends: adrift on loving's sea that laves
our rocky coasts, we clash; no sunken doom
our meeting brings: the surge our bodies saves,
and ocean currents buoy: our splash of sea
and air I hear in love's unspoken words.
Through swells from smashing rocks I plied my oars,
now we in passion clash our craggy shores.

SKYLLA

The form that Kirke drew too swiftly struck:
from whirlpool's depths my eyes I pulled and cast
above; six dangling men accursed by luck
I saw; by two unjointed legs held fast,
each fed a maw of tripled teeth: vain thought
with arms to curb foul Skylla's appetite.
When me with waving arms you reach to pluck,
my self I gladly give, my love at last
your meal: in clutching coils of you I'm stuck
till you my body raise; then I slip past
your lips, by hungry mouths of you soon caught:
with flesh I feed your loving appetite.
Then anguished cries I heard as Skylla ate,
now passioned sighs I cry as you I sate.

HELIOS' CATTLE

A month of landward gales our stores devoured:
the fear of famine gnawed my crew; I slept
alone and woke to find the herd deflow'red;
on spits the cattle lowed, and cowhide crept
the ground; a week's grim feast bright Helios gave:
my ship was split by Zeus with angry bolt.
The wrath of gods I face by you empow'red,
my living's hungry gnaw: my soul adept
the crags has climbed, and stormy waters scoured
in quest of food; and bitter tears I've wept
from famine's pains; but you my seeking save:
my stomach soul still burns from loving's bolt.
My crew with lightning death their feeding paid,
with you I live, my hunger never stayed.

KHARYBDIS

The hungry jaws in cave of death could wait:
for sucking maelstrom's pull now I could feel,
and heard the rocks and sand in swirling grate;
from billow sprung to bough, I watched my keel
the funnel black descend: at dusk disgorged,
astride I leaped, and fled with rowing hands.
No fear I feel to ply your narrow strait:
your mouths I've fed, now swim your whirling wheel
of waves; in seas of you I plunge, my fate
to seek; above, the closing waters seal
the open vortex hole: by you engorged,
I plumb your swirling depths with clutching hands.
From whirlpool's drowning doom I swiftly rowed,
now deep in you by passion's tide I'm towed.

RETURN TO ITHAKA

By dawn my many-voyaged tale I'd told:
that night they plowed the waves, and me ashore
in silence, sleeping soft, they laid, with gold
that shamed the loot of Troy; in grief once more
I woke: my land long years unseen I could not see
till you my sight made clear: I kissed my earth.
Each journey's end to shore of you I'm rolled
by breaking waves and foaming surf's loud roar:
then me in sleeping softness you enfold
as seas recede; your land I've seen before:
not gifted gold, but treasure still to me:
once more with joy I wake and kiss your earth.
At night, asleep, I came to unknown home,
awake, to loving land of you I roam.

EUMAIOS' HUT: REUNION WITH TELEMAKHOS

In loyal swineherd's hut unknown, sweet rest
I found: kind words, then food and cloak he gave;
next day by son's return my life was blest;
my youth restored, a god I seemed, in grave
not doomed to lie: no god but man whose loss
his life had grieved, I wept in son's embrace.
From stormy seas and rocky hills your nest
I seek, and peace: my weary soul you save
from pain of strife, restore my living's zest;
my strength renewed, I yearn the path and wave
of life to ply: no god but man whose dross
is skimmed by you, I rise from love's embrace.
With grieving arms I found my son anew,
in loving arms I find my self in you.

THE BEGGAR

A beggar wrapped in rags to manor came:
my voice old Argos, cast in dung, did hear,
then died; in hall no welcome guest, the shame
of suitors' scorn I bore; 'neath Iros' ear
I plied my fist and shattered jaw: what gall,
in manor mine on bitter scraps to feed.
Now clad in robes of love my right I claim
to feast in halls of you: with welcome cheer
your portals open wide; your tables tame
my hungry heart with foods to fill a year,
and wine to quench my thirsting soul; no pall
your manor dims: on your sweet love I feed.
With beggar's pangs I passed through manor gate,
in lover's hall I feast from brimming plate.

THE WARRIOR'S CLOTHING

In beggar's guise my wife a tale I told:
her man long years ago I'd seen: he wore
a fleecy purple cloak with brooch of gold –
a hound with dappled fawn held fast it bore –
and tunic fine as onion's sheen; salt tears
she wept: with her own hands her man she'd clothed.
Our love the living clothes of you enfold:
your hair a flowing cloak our heat to store;
your skin a tunic fit our flesh to hold;
your limbs a brooch – engraved with passion's lore –
our bodies close to clasp: thus we long years
together lie, our life by loving clothed.
My clothes though long outworn moved wife to cry,
now clad in clothes of you with love we sigh.

EURYKLEIA: THE SCAR

No foolish maid I'd have to bathe my feet,
but wise old servant sought: in sudden fear
I turned away – again I felt the heat
of slashing tusk of boar – lest truth appear
to knowing eyes; too late: my name she sighed
as scar on thigh she touched with tracing hand.
From bath of you my body shuns retreat;
it seeks your woman wise: when you I near
no doubt I feel, but passion's pulsing beat
and burning fire; inside my soul you peer
with knowing eyes: then me with flowing tide
you bathe, and body trace with touching hand.
I turned in fear when servant bathed my feet,
with love I feel our bathing bodies meet.

PENELOPE'S CUNNING: THE BOW

My loving, witted wife for suitors ploys
devised: by day a shroud she wove, at night
the loom undid; then made those heroes boys:
who could my bow re-string, and arrow sight,
her hand would win; the bow all failed in shame:
the string I plucked and shot the arrow true.
Your cunning skills of love my soul enjoys:
on loom of me you weave, a cloak of light
with yarn of sun and moon; you bear no toys
for games, but lover's arms: my arrow flight
is sure, my bow you bend with ease: you tame
my tauten'd string, shoot me with loving true.
To me my wife my bow with love restored,
by you am I through love an arrow soared.

THE SLAUGHTER OF THE SUITORS

To suitors unexpected gifts I gave,
their vengeful host: to first my arrow flew,
his throat a fountain bled; to others, wave
of doom: with son and herdsmen scores I slew:
their sides we pierced with spears, and hacked their flesh
with swords: no bride their arms embraced, but death.
On battlefield ourselves with love we save
when arms we bear: our loving weapons true
to passion's war, our spirits fill no grave;
to piercing eye we give unshielded view;
in clasping arms our bodies bare we mesh:
our battle ends with life embraced, not death.
With vengeful wrath the suitors' blood I spilled,
my loving war with you in peace is stilled.

THE PURGING OF THE HALL

In bloody gore I stood, the suitors slain:
the wailing sluts the hacked-up corpses bore,
then washed the tables, chairs; the clotted stain
my son and herdsmen scraped from earthen floor:
before I washed the blood from legs and arms,
the hall I purged of death with cleansing fire.
My body lies in pools of living's pain,
by grief and woe cut down: your balm you pour
and wash my wounds, your gentle, cleaning rain;
then me you bear with healing arms before
my heart to death succumbs; I live your charms:
my soul you cleanse of doom with loving fire.
From bloody death with flames I purged my hall,
now you to life my self with love recall.

THE OLIVE TREE BED

Penelope denied the servant's call
and son's rebuke: we have our secret signs:
I met her test, enraged at sleep in hall:
'round olive tree I'd laid our bedroom's lines,
then trunk I'd hewn and planed, our sign I'd wrought:
again we touched, then talked, in secret bed.
We meet at end of daily strife, at fall
of dark: and then our secret softly shines,
no longer held from view; within our wall
of love we grow around ourselves like vines,
and share the sign we kept in silent thought:
each night we touch and talk in loving bed.
The bed I'd made was sign for wife's last test,
in bed we make our secret's place of rest.

LAERTES AND HIS LINE

My father's grief I stilled when I appeared:
the manor hall he'd left for lonely plot:
his single son lay dead he thought, and feared
for grandson's life: to die unmourned his lot
would be; but we his eye made glad: he joyed
to see our strength, his blood's ongoing line.
What grieving men I've seen whose lives were steered
by birth of single son; their joys were not
to be: their sons by fate's grim reaper sheared
from growth, in living graves with weeping rot
their hopes; but you my heart make glad: I'm buoyed
by second son, my life's ongoing line.
Laertes' line was famed for being one,
now mine is spread by birth of second son.

VICTORY

Through twenty years of war on sea and land
I fought with men and waves: and then I moored,
an aged paltry thing, unfit to stand,
till you my beard made black, my limbs restored;
the suitors died; my wife and son regained,
I wore my crown: again you gave me life.
I'll not begin to count these years at hand,
the days of wars and seas to you I'll hoard:
a country meant for me whom age unmanned,
you heal the bruise of wind and wound of sword;
ashore by you, my mind and body, stained
with tears, awake from weary age to life.
You stopped the certain course of life's decay,
now daily flow of sand and blood you stay.

PEACE FROM THE GODS

The suitors' kin a bloody vengeance sought,
but gods on mountain high a halt decreed:
you spoke to Zeus, and blameless end he wrought –
their memories erased, my honor's need
fulfilled: his bolt soon checked my wrath's last cry,
your warning words to warring soul gave peace.
Whatever fate the gods to me have brought,
I face my living's end with peace: I feed
on memories of bloody wars I've fought
and stormy seas I've sailed; for you I heed
whose voice has been my call to life: to my
contending soul your loving words bring peace.
Your warning words restrained my warring strife,
with loving words you've eased my soul through life.

EPILOGUE:

THE GODDESS FORSAKES ODYSSEUS

A wind-maned wave it was, up-rearing,
that spilled us, bow over stern,
into the sea;
I felt his sea-shaking hooves from afar,
and saw his spray-cloud over my shoulder,
but it was too late even then.
It rained so hard, and the wind blew,
that I scarce knew I was under water.
My hand reached out, grasped:
clutched and held the flying tail;
I was torn up and out –
in the bursting forth
my lungs near exploded with gasping
and my head with crying out your name,
but the rain filled my mouth
quickly as the sea emptied it,
and my voice drowned,
soundless –
only to plunge even deeper this time
(though by now I had let go),
and his tail lashed my face
as his hooves pummeled my lungs:

no dream, this, no illusion,
no music of minstrels;
no wife to see me off,
nor son to welcome me;
my comrades gone ahead,
alone, no goddess to guide me,
I am not even granted my third going down.

Athena!
Can your bright eyes see into the green foam?
Find mine flashing proudly for the last time? –
He had to seek me beyond the Pillars of Hercules!